Level B • Book 1

QuickReads®
A Research-Based Fluency Program

Elfrieda H. Hiebert, Ph.D.

MODERN CURRICULUM PRESS

Pearson Learning Group

Program Reviewers and Consultants

Dr. Barbara A. Baird
Director of Federal Programs/Richardson ISD
Richardson, TX

Dr. Kate Kinsella
Dept. of Secondary Education and Step to College Program
San Francisco State University
San Francisco, CA

Pat Sears
Early Child Coordinator/Virginia Beach Public Schools
Virginia Beach, VA

Dr. Judith B. Smith
Supervisor of ESOL and World and Classical Languages/Baltimore City Public Schools
Baltimore, MD

The following people have contributed to the development of this product:

Art and Design: Adriano Farinella, Dorothea Fox, Salita Mehta,
 Janice Noto-Helmers, Evelyn O'Shea, Dan Thomas

Editorial: Lynn W. Kloss

Manufacturing: Michele Uhl

Marketing: Connie Buck

Production: Laura Benford-Sullivan, Jeffrey Engel

Publishing Operations: Jennifer Van Der Heide

Modern
Curriculum
Press

Pearson Learning Group

1-800-321-3106
www.pearsonlearning.com

Contents

SOCIAL STUDIES

National Symbols

Contents

SOCIAL STUDIES

Brave Americans

Contents

SCIENCE **Insects**

Contents

Acknowledgments

All photographs © Pearson Learning unless otherwise noted

Cover: Dale O'Dell/Stock Connection/PictureQuest.

Interior: 3: Corbis Digital Stock. 4: Bob Daemmrich/Stock Boston. 5: NASA. 6: © John M. Burnley/National Audubon Society/Photo Researchers, Inc. 7: Christoph Burki/Getty Images, Inc. 8: Thomas Kitchin/Tom Stack & Associates. 10: Bob Daemmrich/Stock Boston, Inc./PictureQuest. 12: Corbis Digital Stock. 14: Tony Freeman/PhotoEdit. 16: Michio Hoshino/Minden Pictures. 18: Bob Daemmrich/Stock Boston. 24: © Ariel Skelley/Corbis. 26: Bill Bachman/PhotoEdit. 28: Michael Newman/PhotoEdit. 30: Gale Zucker/Stock Boston. 32: Richard Nowitz/Photo Researchers, Inc. 38: NASA. 40: Getty Images, Inc. 42: Corbis. 44: AP/Wide World Photos. 46: American Foundation for the Blind. 52: Frans Lanting/Minden Pictures. 54: Lena Untidt/Bonnier Publications/Science Photo Library/Photo Researchers, Inc. 56: Graeme Ellis-Ursus/Ursus Photography, Vancouver. 58: Myrleen Ferguson/PhotoEdit. 60: John M. Burnley/National Audubon Society/Photo Researchers, Inc. 66: Bruce Davidson/Animals Animals/Earth Scenes. 68: Christoph Burki/Getty Images, Inc. 70: Grant Heilman Photography, Inc. 72: Dinodia/Omni-Photo Communications, Inc. 74: Jeff Greenberg/PhotoEdit. 82: Thomas Kitchin/Tom Stack & Associates, Inc. 84: Ken Biggs/Getty Images, Inc. 88: George Godfrey/Earth Scenes.

National Symbols

The flag is a symbol of freedom in the United States.

Symbols of the United States

You have seen the flag flying at your school. You can see pictures of the bald eagle on money. The[25] flag and the bald eagle are symbols of the United States. When we see these symbols, we think about things that are important to our[50] country.

Freedom was important to the people who started this country. They wanted freedom for everyone. When we see symbols like the flag and the[75] bald eagle, we think about things that are important to the people of the United States, like freedom[93].

National Symbols

The stars and stripes on the flag are symbols
of the states of the United States.

Stars and Stripes

Sometimes the flag of the United States is called the "Stars and Stripes." A look at the flag will tell you why.[25] The flag has a block of stars. Each star stands for a state in the United States. Every time a new state was added to[50] the United States, a star was added to the flag. The flag now has 50 stars.

There are also stripes on the flag. The number[75] of stripes stays the same. Each stripe stands for one of the first 13 states in the United States.[94]

National Symbols

Red, white, and blue are
symbols used on July 4th.

Red, White, and Blue

If you like a sports team, you know that the team always wears the same colors. Colors can also be symbols.[25] People who want to show they like a sports team wear the colors of that team.

The colors red, white, and blue are symbols of[50] the United States. These are the colors on the flag. On July 4th, people in the United States fly red, white, and blue flags on[75] their houses. People also wear red, white, and blue on July 4th to show they love the United States.[94]

National Symbols

The bald eagle is another symbol
of the United States.

Bald Eagle

The bald eagle is our country's bird. The bald eagle was picked because it is a strong and beautiful bird. The bald eagle[25] is a symbol of the United States.

The bald eagle is not really bald. It has white feathers on its head. The rest of the[50] bald eagle's feathers are dark. People used to hunt bald eagles. In the 1970s, there were not many bald eagles left. Laws were passed to[75] keep bald eagles safe. Now there are four times as many bald eagles as there were in the 1970s.[94]

National Symbols

Many students begin their school day
by saying the Pledge of Allegiance.

The Pledge of Allegiance

Your school day may begin with the Pledge of Allegiance. When you say the Pledge of Allegiance, you put your right[25] hand over your heart. You look at the flag, which is a symbol of freedom. Then you say the Pledge of Allegiance.

The Pledge of[50]Allegiance is a symbol, too. You put your hand over your heart because you are saying that you love your country. No one has to[75]say the Pledge of Allegiance. Yet everyone can say the Pledge of Allegiance. That is another symbol of freedom[94].

National Symbols

Write words that will help you remember what you learned.

Symbols of the United States

_____

_____

_____

_____

Stars and Stripes

_____

_____

_____

_____

Red, White, and Blue

_____

_____

_____

_____

Bald Eagle

_____

_____

_____

_____

The Pledge of Allegiance

_____

_____

_____

_____

Symbols of the United States

1. The main idea of "Symbols of the United States" is that _____

   Ⓐ the flag at school has a bald eagle on it.

   Ⓑ every country needs a flag.

   Ⓒ the bald eagle is the only symbol of the United States.

   Ⓓ symbols make us think about things that are important.

2. What two symbols of the United States did you learn about in this reading?

_____

_____

_____

Stars and Stripes

1. Another good name for "Stars and Stripes" is _____

   Ⓐ "Fifty States."

   Ⓑ "Our Country's Flag."

   Ⓒ "Stars in the Flag."

   Ⓓ "The Many States of the United States."

2. What do the stars and stripes in the flag stand for?

_____

_____

_____

Red, White, and Blue

1. "Red, White, and Blue" is MAINLY about _____

Ⓐ why sports teams wear the same colors.

Ⓑ what people do on July 4th.

Ⓒ the colors red, white, and blue as symbols of the United States.

Ⓓ the many different symbols of the United States.

2. Why do people wear red, white, and blue?

_____

_____

_____

Bald Eagle

1. Why was the bald eagle picked as our country's bird?

Ⓐ It is a strong and beautiful bird.

Ⓑ It has blue and white feathers.

Ⓒ It is the most famous bird in the United States.

Ⓓ It is only found in the United States.

2. What happened to the bald eagle from the 1970s to today?

_____

_____

_____

The Pledge of Allegiance

1. The Pledge of Allegiance is a symbol of _____

   Ⓐ a person's love of the United States.

   Ⓑ the bald eagle and the flag.

   Ⓒ school rules.

   Ⓓ the colors red, white, and blue.

2. What do you do when you say the Pledge of Allegiance?

   _____

   _____

   _____

Connect Your Ideas

1. Tell about two symbols of the United States.

   _____

   _____

   _____

2. Which symbol do you think is the best symbol of the United States? Why?

   _____

   _____

   _____

Being a Citizen

Children in the United States
have the right to go to school.

The Rights of Citizens

You are a citizen of your school. You are also a citizen of your town, state, and country. Citizens in the[25] United States have rights. Rights are the things you can do. No one can take away your rights as a citizen.

You have the right[50] to go to school. You have the right to go to the park or ride on a bus. When you grow up, you will have[75] the right to vote. People in the United States have the right to vote for anyone they choose.[93]

Being a Citizen

One responsibility citizens have is
following the rules of their town.

The Responsibilities of Citizens

Citizens have both rights and responsibilities. Responsibilities are jobs that you need to do. As a citizen of your school, you[25] have responsibilities at school. You need to do your work. You need to be nice to other people.

As a citizen of your town, you[50] have responsibilities in your town. You need to put your trash in a trashcan. You need to follow the rules of your town.

As a[75] citizen of your country, you have responsibilities, too. When you grow up, you will have the responsibility to vote.[94]

Being a Citizen

You can speak up for your rights
if someone tries to bully you.

Speak Up for Your Rights

As a citizen of your school, you have the right to learn. You also have the right to be safe.[25] Sometimes, someone at your school might act like a bully. A bully might tease or hurt you so that it is hard to learn or[50] to feel safe. A bully wants to take away your rights.

You need to speak up for your rights. If a bully is mean to[75] you, you can walk away. You can say, "Stop!" You can also ask a teacher for help.[92]

Being a Citizen

Citizens can work together to
make a neighborhood park.

Making a Better Neighborhood

Good citizens try to fix problems. James Ale was nine years old when he saw a problem in his town. There[25] was no park in James's neighborhood. Children played ball in the street. One day, a car hit a boy. The boy got better. Yet James[50] wanted a park in his neighborhood.

James wrote letters to the leaders in his town. He talked with the leaders in his town. At last,[75] the town made a park in James's neighborhood. James was a good citizen. He helped fix a problem.[93]

Being a Citizen

Children can work together to
fix a problem in their town.

A Class of Good Citizens

Like James Ale, a class of fifth graders saw a problem. A man had a trash dump next to their[25] school. Some days the trash dump smelled bad. On those days, it was hard for children to learn.

The fifth graders and their teacher talked[50] about how to fix the problem. They did what good citizens do. The class wrote letters to the leaders of their town. Because of the[75] letters, the town's leaders told the man to fix the trash dump. These fifth graders were good citizens.[93]

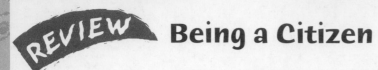

Write words that will help you remember what you learned.

The Rights of Citizens

_____

_____

_____

_____

The Responsibilities of Citizens

_____

_____

_____

_____

Speak Up for Your Rights

_____

_____

_____

_____

Making a Better Neighborhood

_____

_____

_____

_____

A Class of Good Citizens

_____

_____

_____

_____

The Rights of Citizens

1. What are rights?

   Ⓐ the citizens in your school

   Ⓑ the people you vote for

   Ⓒ the things you can do

   Ⓓ the country where you live

2. What are some rights you have as a citizen of the United States?

_____

_____

_____

The Responsibilities of Citizens

1. What are responsibilities?

   Ⓐ things you can do

   Ⓑ trash in a trashcan

   Ⓒ citizens who have rights

   Ⓓ jobs you need to do

2. What are some responsibilities you have as a citizen?

_____

_____

_____

Being a Citizen

Speak Up for Your Rights

1. "Speak Up for Your Rights" is MAINLY about _____

   Ⓐ how to be safe from a bully.

   Ⓑ how to stop being a bully.

   Ⓒ why bullies take away other people's rights.

   Ⓓ when to talk to your teacher.

2. How could you stand up for your rights if someone bullied you?

   _____

   _____

   _____

Making a Better Neighborhood

1. Another name for "Making a Better Neighborhood" might be _____

   Ⓐ "Citizens Can Fix Problems."

   Ⓑ "Writing Letters."

   Ⓒ "Problems in Town."

   Ⓓ "Neighborhoods Need Parks."

2. What problem did James Ale solve in his neighborhood?

   _____

   _____

   _____

A Class of Good Citizens

1. What problem did the fifth graders have in "A Class of Good Citizens"?

    Ⓐ They did not know how to write letters.

    Ⓑ There was no trash dump near their school.

    Ⓒ A trash dump near their school smelled bad.

    Ⓓ A man fixed the trash dump near their school.

2. How did the fifth grade class fix its problem?

    _____

    _____

    _____

Connect Your Ideas

1. Name two rights and two responsibilities of a citizen.

    _____

    _____

    _____

2. What problem would you like to fix in your neighborhood? How could you try to fix it?

    _____

    _____

    _____

Brave Americans

Sally Ride was the first American
woman to ride in space.

Sally Ride

Sally Ride was the first American woman in space. She had a great name for a person who took a ride in space![25] From the time she was young, Sally Ride liked to learn about space.

She worked hard to learn the jobs of astronauts. She learned the[50] jobs so well that she was picked to go on trips into space two times. When Sally Ride got back from her last ride in[75] space she said, "The thing that I'll remember most about being an astronaut is that it was fun."[93]

Brave Americans

Abraham Lincoln helped to end slavery.

Abraham Lincoln

When he was young, Abraham Lincoln was too poor to go to school. He learned to read and write by himself. His hard[25] work helped him become President of the United States.

Soon after Lincoln became president, a war started between Americans in the north and south. Lincoln[50] did not want the people of the United States to go to war. However, the north and south did go to war. One thing people[75] went to war about was slavery. Lincoln knew that slavery was not right. President Lincoln helped to end slavery.[94]

Brave Americans

Sitting Bull worked to help
his people keep their land.

Sitting Bull

In 1868, the United States told a group of Native Americans that they could live in the Black Hills forever. Then gold was[25] found in the Black Hills. The United States wanted the Native Americans to sell their land. However, the Native Americans did not want to leave[50] their homes.

A war started between the United States and these Native Americans. Sitting Bull led the Native Americans. They lost the war. Sitting Bull's[75] people had to leave their homes. Because he tried to help his people, Sitting Bull was a brave American.[94]

George Washington Carver showed
poor farmers how to make more money.

George Washington Carver

George Washington Carver was a scientist who knew about plants. He learned that soil wears out when farmers grow the same crop[25] every year. When soil wears out, crops are poor. George Washington Carver told farmers how to grow one crop in one year. Then they would[50] grow a different crop in the next year.

George Washington Carver also found more than 300 ways to use peanuts. When farmers planted peanuts, they[75] could sell their crops and make money. George Washington Carver was a great scientist who helped poor farmers.[93]

Brave Americans

Helen Keller learned to read by using
her hands on special books.

Helen Keller

When Helen Keller was a very small child, she lost her sight and her hearing. However, these handicaps did not keep Helen Keller[25] from learning to read, write, and speak.

Helen Keller learned about words when her teacher put her hand in water. Her teacher spelled the word[50] *water* by tapping on Helen's hand.

Helen Keller read and wrote in special ways, yet she learned to read and write very well. She spoke[75] to many groups of people. Helen Keller did not let her handicaps stop her from doing things.[92]

Brave Americans

Write words that will help you remember what you learned.

Sally Ride

_____

_____

_____

_____

Abraham Lincoln

_____

_____

_____

_____

Sitting Bull

_____

_____

_____

_____

George Washington Carver

_____

_____

_____

_____

Helen Keller

_____

_____

_____

_____

Sally Ride

1. Another good name for "Sally Ride" is _____

   Ⓐ "Space Explorers."

   Ⓑ "A Trip to Space."

   Ⓒ "How to Become an Astronaut."

   Ⓓ "The First American Woman in Space."

2. How did Sally Ride become an astronaut?

_____

_____

_____

Abraham Lincoln

1. Which of these sentences best tells about Abraham Lincoln?

   Ⓐ Abraham Lincoln tried to start the war.

   Ⓑ Abraham Lincoln was a brave president.

   Ⓒ Abraham Lincoln tried to live in the United States.

   Ⓓ Abraham Lincoln was a brave student.

2. What two important things did Abraham Lincoln do?

_____

_____

_____

Brave Americans

Sitting Bull

1. Why is Sitting Bull a brave American?

   Ⓐ He found gold in the Black Hills.

   Ⓑ He left his home.

   Ⓒ He saved his people's home in the Black Hills.

   Ⓓ He tried to help his people keep their land.

2. Why did a war begin between Sitting Bull's people and the United States?

   _____

   _____

   _____

George Washington Carver

1. The main idea of "George Washington Carver" is _____

   Ⓐ that he was a scientist who helped farmers.

   Ⓑ that he showed farmers how to become scientists.

   Ⓒ that he knew every plant.

   Ⓓ that he showed farmers how to make peanuts.

2. Name two ways George Washington Carver helped farmers.

   _____

   _____

   _____

Helen Keller

1. "Helen Keller" is MAINLY about ____

   Ⓐ how Helen Keller did not let handicaps stop her from doing things.

   Ⓑ how Helen Keller lost her sight and her hearing.

   Ⓒ the new words Helen Keller used.

   Ⓓ how Helen Keller learned to speak.

2. How did Helen Keller overcome her handicaps?

   _____

   _____

   _____

Connect Your Ideas

1. Tell about how two of these brave Americans are like each other.

   _____

   _____

   _____

2. What do you think makes a person brave?

   _____

   _____

   _____

Do Animals Talk?

Some birds communicate by moving their tails.

How Animals Communicate

Animals don't talk, but they do communicate. When you communicate, you give information to others. Animals have ways of communicating that are [25] different from the ways that people use. When your friend talks to you, your friend uses language to communicate information. In a language, each word [50] means something.

Animals do not use words. They use sounds and signals. Birds sing and move their wings. Some animals move their tails. Other animals [75] communicate by moving their bodies in other ways. Different sounds and signals help animals communicate with each other. [93]

Do Animals Talk?

The lines in this picture show how
honeybees move when they dance.

The Honeybee Dance

One way honeybees communicate with each other is by dancing. Honeybees do a special dance after they find nectar in flowers. Honeybees[25] need nectar to live. When honeybees find nectar, they fly home to tell the other bees where to find the nectar.

A bee that finds[50] nectar moves its wings very fast when it dances. The bee moves in a shape that looks like the number 8. The bee does the[75] dance many times. After the dance, the other bees know where to find the flowers with nectar.[92]

Humpback whales can sing for a long time.

Whales

Whales communicate with each other by singing. Different kinds of whales sing different songs. Whales in different parts of the world sing different songs,[25] too. When a whale sings, people can sometimes hear the sound. However, people near a singing whale can also feel the water move from the[50] sound.

When most kinds of whales communicate with each other, the song is short. Yet when a humpback whale sings, it sings only for itself.[75] It also can sing for a long time. A humpback whale can sing for twenty minutes at a time.[94]

Do Animals Talk?

Dogs can show they are friendly by wagging their tails and by sitting close to people.

Dogs

A bark is a sound a dog makes to communicate something to people or other animals. A bark can be a friendly way to[25] say "hi." Sometimes dogs bark to tell their owners that they see people they do not know. Sometimes dogs bark to scare other dogs.

Dogs[50] also communicate by moving their bodies. Dogs show their teeth when they are upset. They wag their tails when they are happy. They wag their[75] tails when their owners give them food. Dogs also wag their tails when their owners take them for walks.[94]

Danger signals help prairie dogs stay safe.

Danger Signals

People have danger signals to tell others to be careful. Signs at a train crossing and stop signs keep us from danger. Animals[25] have danger signals to keep them safe, too.

Some animals make sounds that tell other animals to be careful. When prairie dogs think there is[50] danger, they call to each other in a certain way. The danger might be bigger animals that want to catch the prairie dogs. The prairie[75] dog's call tells other prairie dogs that a big animal is coming. This call says, "Be careful!"[92]

Do Animals Talk?

Write words that will help you remember what you learned.

How Animals Communicate

_____

_____

_____

_____

The Honeybee Dance

_____

_____

_____

_____

Whales

_____

_____

_____

_____

Dogs

_____

_____

_____

_____

Danger Signals

_____

_____

_____

_____

How Animals Communicate

1. "How Animals Communicate" is MAINLY about _____
   - Ⓐ words animals can learn.
   - Ⓑ how animals use sounds and signals to communicate.
   - Ⓒ how animals use language to communicate.
   - Ⓓ how people communicate with animals.

2. How do animals communicate?

   _____

   _____

   _____

The Honeybee Dance

1. Why do honeybees dance?
   - Ⓐ to find honeycombs
   - Ⓑ to find the other bees
   - Ⓒ to fly home
   - Ⓓ to communicate with one another

2. How do honeybees dance?

   _____

   _____

   _____

Do Animals Talk?

Whales

1. Another good name for "Whales" is _____
   - Ⓐ "How Whales Communicate."
   - Ⓑ "Different Kinds of Whales."
   - Ⓒ "Humpback Whales."
   - Ⓓ "Songs You Can't Hear."

2. Retell two important facts you learned in "Whales."

   _____

   _____

   _____

Dogs

1. Why do dogs bark?
   - Ⓐ to communicate with people or other animals
   - Ⓑ to find food
   - Ⓒ to find other dogs
   - Ⓓ to tell where they are

2. What are two ways dogs communicate?

   _____

   _____

   _____

Danger Signals

1. The main idea of "Danger Signals" is that ____

    Ⓐ signs at train crossings keep people safe.

    Ⓑ animals need humans to keep them safe.

    Ⓒ people and animals use danger signals to keep them safe.

    Ⓓ all animals use the same sounds to keep them safe.

2. Why do prairie dogs use danger signals?

_____

_____

_____

Connect Your Ideas

1. Name two ways animals use to communicate with one another.

_____

_____

_____

2. Why do animals communicate with each other?

_____

_____

_____

Goliath beetles are large insects
that have feelers and wings.

What Is an Insect?

A flea can be so small that you might not see it land on this page. A Goliath beetle can be[25] as long as half of this page. Fleas and Goliath beetles are different in size, but they are both insects.

Many insects have feelers for[50] smelling and wings for flying. However, some insects do not have feelers and wings.

How are insects the same? All insects have six legs and[75] a three-part body. This means that fleas and Goliath beetles have six legs and three-part bodies.[93]

Insects

The shells of ladybugs are red with black dots.

An Animal with No Bones

Without bones, people would be like jam. Bones help people walk and stand. Insects don't have any bones inside their[25] bodies. Yet they can fly, crawl, or jump. How do they do it?

In place of bones, insects have a hard shell on the outside[50] of their body. The hard shell makes insects strong. It keeps their soft, inside parts safe. The hard shells of many insects are beautiful. Ladybugs[75] have a red shell with black dots. Their shells make it easy to find ladybugs resting on flowers.[93]

Ants move by crawling.

How Insects Move

Most insects have wings. Other than birds and bats, insects are the only animals that can fly. Insects fly at different speeds.[25] One kind of fly goes 35 miles an hour. Houseflies go five miles an hour. That's still fast when you are trying to catch a[50] housefly!

Insects without wings jump or crawl. One kind of flea can jump more than one foot into the air. Other insects crawl, such as[75] cockroaches and ants. One kind of cockroach can crawl three miles an hour. That's fast for a small insect.[94]

Insects

This insect is sitting on a leaf.

Where Insects Live

When you play in a park, 500 to 2,000 insects may be around you. Some are underground. Others are on plants or[25] trees. You might not see many of these insects because insects often look like the rocks or plants around them. A leaf insect looks like[50] a leaf on the trees around it.

There are more insects on Earth than any other kind of animal. Insects live in most places on[75] Earth. Some insects even live in water. The only place without insects is the deep water of the sea.[94]

Insects

Some kinds of insects eat leaves.

How Insects Help and Hurt

When a housefly buzzes around your head at night, it's a pest! Some insect pests can hurt plants, animals, and [25] people. Flies can carry germs that make people sick. Ticks can feed on animals and even people. Some kinds of insects eat farmers' crops.

However, [50] many insects are helpful to plants, animals, and people. Ladybugs eat the greenflies that eat plants. Without ladybugs, some plants would be eaten by greenflies. [75] Many beetles eat dead things like leaves. By doing this, they help the farmers' crops to grow. [92]

Write words that will help you remember what you learned.

What Is an Insect?

_____

_____

_____

_____

An Animal with No Bones

_____

_____

_____

_____

How Insects Move

_____

_____

_____

_____

Where Insects Live

_____

_____

_____

_____

How Insects Help and Hurt

_____

_____

_____

_____

What Is an Insect?

1. How are all insects the same?

   Ⓐ All insects are small.

   Ⓑ All insects have feelers and six legs.

   Ⓒ All insects have a three-part body and six legs.

   Ⓓ All insects have feelers and wings.

2. How can insects be different?

   _____

   _____

   _____

An Animal with No Bones

1. Another good name for "An Animal With No Bones" is _____

   Ⓐ "An Insect's Shell."

   Ⓑ "How Insects Grow Bones."

   Ⓒ "Inside an Insect."

   Ⓓ "Why People Need Bones."

2. What does an insect's shell do?

   _____

   _____

   _____

How Insects Move

1. In what ways can insects move?

  Ⓐ They can ride on the wind.

  Ⓑ They can fly, swim, and roll.

  Ⓒ They can travel on other animals' backs.

  Ⓓ They can fly, jump, and crawl.

2. Retell two facts you learned in "How Insects Move."

_____

_____

_____

Where Insects Live

1. "Where Insects Live" is MAINLY about _____

  Ⓐ the plants insects live on.

  Ⓑ how insects make homes.

  Ⓒ where insects live on Earth and in water.

  Ⓓ how insects live inside the earth.

2. Where do insects live?

_____

_____

_____

How Insects Help and Hurt

1. How can insects hurt people?

    Ⓐ by carrying germs that make people sick

    Ⓑ by eating greenflies

    Ⓒ by eating your food

    Ⓓ by feeding on animals

2. Name two ways insects can help you.

_____

_____

_____

Connect Your Ideas

1. List two facts you learned about insects.

_____

_____

_____

2. Suppose there was another reading. Do you think it would be about beetles or about birds? Why?

_____

_____

_____

Trees

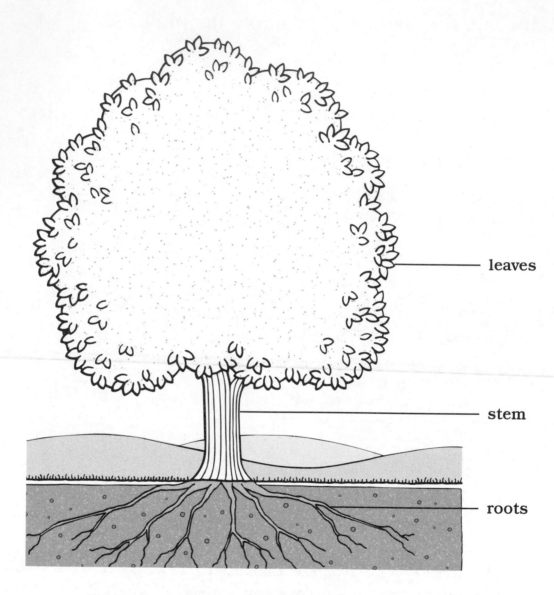

leaves

stem

roots

Trees have leaves, stems, and roots.

80

What Is a Tree?

There are many kinds of trees, but all trees are big plants. Like all plants, trees have roots. The roots hold[25] trees in the ground. The roots soak up the water and food that trees need to live.

A tree has a fat stem to hold[50] it up. The fat stem is called the tree's trunk. Inside the trunk, a tree holds water and food. The water and food go up[75] the trunk to the green leaves. The leaves of a tree use sunlight to make more food for the tree.[95]

Trees

Pinecones hold the seeds of new pine trees.

Make a Guess

It has cones but no ice cream. It has bark but it's not a dog. It has needles but the needles are[25] not used to sew things. Can you guess what it is? You are right if you guessed it is a pine tree.

Pine trees have[50] cones. A pinecone is hard and brown with seeds inside. When the seeds drop on the ground, a new tree can grow. Pine trees have[75] thick bark. The leaves of pine trees look like needles. A pine tree's needles are long, thin, and green.[94]

Trees

Redwoods are giant trees.

The Giants of Trees

Redwood trees are the giants of trees. One giant redwood tree is more than 350 feet high and 44 feet around.[25] Redwood trees are so big that it would take more than 20 children to hug one. That is one giant hug!

It takes a long[50] time for a redwood tree to grow to be a giant. Most trees live fewer than 100 years. However, a redwood tree can live more[75] than 2,000 years. No other tree can live as long or grow as big as a redwood.[92]

Water moves through trees in the same
way as it moves through celery.

How Water Moves Through Trees

You can't see inside a tree. Yet you can study how water moves through trees. First, get a stalk of [25]celery and cut off its end. Put red food color in a cup of water. Then put the stalk of celery into the red water.[50]

After a half hour, take the celery out. Cut it in half. Your celery should be red. This is because the water moved up the[75] stalk. Water moves through trees in the same way as it moved through the celery.[90]

Rings show how trees have grown.

Rings in Trees

When a tree is cut down, you can see circles in its stump. These circles are called rings. These rings show how[25] trees have grown each year. Trees make one ring each year. Trees that have ten rings are ten years old. Trees that have 200 rings[50] are 200 years old.

Each ring shows how much a tree grew in one year. A ring will be fat if there was lots of[75] water that year. Some tree rings are thin because there was not much water that year.[91]

 **Trees**

Write words that will help you remember what you learned.

What Is a Tree?	Make a Guess
_____	_____
_____	_____
_____	_____
_____	_____

The Giants of Trees	How Water Moves Through Trees
_____	_____
_____	_____
_____	_____
	_____

Rings in Trees

_____

_____

_____

_____

What Is a Tree?

1. "What Is a Tree?" MAINLY tells about _____

   Ⓐ different kinds of trees.

   Ⓑ what trees need to live.

   Ⓒ how tall trees are.

   Ⓓ what parts trees have.

2. What are the three parts of a tree?

_____

_____

_____

Make a Guess

1. Another good name for "Make a Guess" is _____

   Ⓐ "Pine Needles."

   Ⓑ "Pine Trees."

   Ⓒ "Trees With Cones."

   Ⓓ "Cones and Needles."

2. How can you tell if a tree is a pine tree?

_____

_____

_____

The Giants of Trees

1. Which of these is a fact about redwood trees?

 Ⓐ They can live for a long time.

 Ⓑ They can live for fewer than 100 years.

 Ⓒ Children often hug them.

 Ⓓ They grow very quickly.

2. Tell about two ways redwood trees are different from other trees.

_____

_____

_____

How Water Moves Through Trees

1. A stalk of celery can show _____

 Ⓐ how a tree's leaves work.

 Ⓑ how a tree's bark works.

 Ⓒ how water moves through trees.

 Ⓓ how trees can be red.

2. How can you show how water moves through trees?

_____

_____

_____

Rings in Trees

1. "Rings in Trees" is MAINLY about ____

   Ⓐ how many years a tree can live.

   Ⓑ which trees have rings.

   Ⓒ how rings in trees show how trees grow.

   Ⓓ which trees have stumps.

2. Retell what you learned about tree rings.

_____

_____

_____

Connect Your Ideas

1. Name three ways that trees can be different from each other.

_____

_____

_____

2. Tell about what trees are and how they live.

_____

_____

_____

Reading Log · Level B · Book 1

	I Read This	New Words I Learned	New Facts I Learned	What Else I Want to Learn About This Subject
National Symbols				
Symbols of the United States				
Stars and Stripes				
Red, White, and Blue				
Bald Eagle				
The Pledge of Allegiance				
Being a Citizen				
The Rights of Citizens				
The Responsibilities of Citizens				
Speak Up for Your Rights				
Making a Better Neighborhood				
A Class of Good Citizens				
Brave Americans				
Sally Ride				
Abraham Lincoln				
Sitting Bull				
George Washington Carver				
Helen Keller				

	I Read This	New Words I Learned	New Facts I Learned	What Else I Want to Learn About This Subject
Do Animals Talk?				
How Animals Communicate				
The Honeybee Dance				
Whales				
Dogs				
Danger Signals				
Insects				
What Is an Insect?				
An Animal with No Bones				
How Insects Move				
Where Insects Live				
How Insects Help and Hurt				
Trees				
What is a Tree?				
Make a Guess				
The Giants of Trees				
How Water Moves Through Trees				
Rings in Trees				

Self-Check Graph

Column headers (reading rates listed vertically):
- Symbols of the United States
- Stars and Stripes
- Red, White, and Blue
- Bald Eagle
- The Pledge of Allegiance
- The Rights of Citizens
- The Responsibilities of Citizens
- Speak Up for Your Rights
- Making a Better Neighborhood
- A Class of Good Citizens
- Sally Ride
- Abraham Lincoln
- Sitting Bull
- George Washington Carver
- Helen Keller
- How Animals Communicate
- The Honeybee Dance
- Whales
- Dogs
- Danger Signals
- What Is an Insect?
- An Animal with No Bones
- How Insects Move
- Where Insects Live
- How Insects Help and Hurt
- What Is a Tree?
- Make a Guess
- The Giants of Trees
- How Water Moves Through Trees
- Rings in Trees

Reading rate scale (left axis): 130, 128, 126, 124, 122, 120, 118, 116, 114, 112, 110, 108, 106, 104, 102, 100, 98, 96, 94, 92, 90, 88, 86, 84, 82, 80, 78, 76, 74, 72, 70, 68, 66, 64, 62, 60, 58, 56, 54, 52, 50

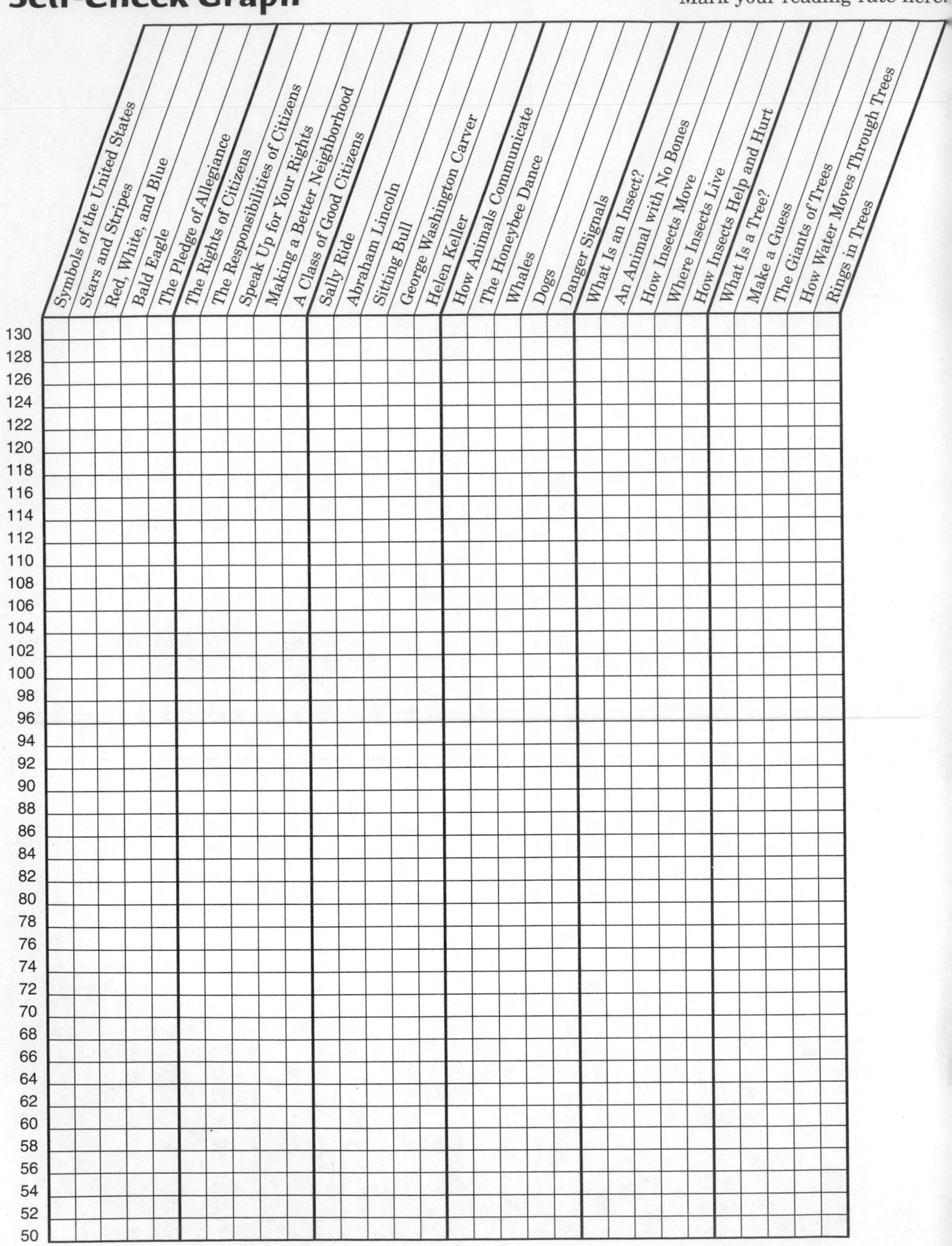